A souvenir guide

Cotehele
Cornwall

8   Later owners

Cotehele House   10
12   Reading Cotehele
15   Make do and mend
16   Tudor Cotehele
18   Civil War Cotehele
22   Georgian Cotehele
24   A royal tour
26   Victorian Cotehele
30   Twentieth-century Cotehele
32   New beginnings

Cotehele's Garland   34

The Garden and Estate   38
39   The garden
44   The orchards
46   The woodland
49   A Cotehele herbal
50   Cotehele Mill

Bound by a River   54
55   Shamrock
56   Cotehele Quay
57   A repeat royal visit
58   Market gardening
59   Salmon fishing
60   Industry on the Tamar

Continuing Inspiration   62
64   Cotehele today

National Trust

The Creation of Cotehele

The River Tamar meanders between Devon and Cornwall. On the Cornish side is Cotehele Quay, once a busy port on which the local community depended. It also served as the gateway to the Edgcumbe family's ancestral home for nearly six centuries.

For centuries, the Tamar Valley has been mined for tin, silver, lead, copper and arsenic. The fertile soil, warm, wet climate and undulating wooded hills have long provided boat builders with a reliable supply of timber, and the sunny slopes have lent themselves to the long-established tradition of growing fruit and flowers, which reached its peak in the 19th century. Boats carried coal and limestone up the Tamar to be burnt as fertilising agent for the farmers' and market gardeners' fields, and the waters teemed with salmon which were fished using nets cast across the river. Given the richness of the land, it's not surprising that Cotehele House should be built in the middle of it. Today, the estate spans 1,300 acres and contains five working farms and 90 cottages.

The house

Although there has been a dwelling at Cotehele since medieval times, the current house is mostly Tudor, rebuilt by three generations of Edgcumbes between 1485 and c.1560, with the interior extensively remodelled during the 1650s.

Between 1547 and 1553, Mount Edgcumbe House was built at West Stonehouse, 12 miles downriver, and became the main family seat. Cotehele was relegated to second-home status before it was even complete. In the mid-18th century Mount Edgcumbe was remodelled, and its outdated furnishings were shipped up the Tamar to Cotehele, where they remain today.

Silhouettes of arms and armour stand out against the austere lime-washed walls of Cotehele's Tudor Hall. In the rooms beyond, a wealth of tapestries enhances the natural dimness of the rooms. The embroideries that adorn the beds, the carved oak chairs, time-worn pewter and brass candlesticks all evoke a sense of antiquity. Composite furnishings such as the King Charles' Room bed, which stands on table legs and is embellished with re-used embroidered panels, bear witness to the Edgcumbes' readiness to

make do and mend. Since the late 18th century, Cotehele has been presented as an ancient family home.

The garden

The garden started to take shape in Victorian times, influenced and inspired by the Dowager Countess, Lady Caroline, who moved to Cotehele in 1862. The horticultural tradition continues today with creativity and flair, and the various gardens within the garden are always changing. Each season has its beauty: in summer, froglets test their new legs, island hopping between the lily pads in the Upper Garden pond; autumn brings vibrant colours and mellow reflections in the Valley Garden and Acer Grove; winter is time to enjoy some seldom-seen river views from the Terraces; but spring, with daffodils, primroses, crocuses and fritillaries, heralds a magical display.

Above The South Range and castellated Gatehouse Tower

Opposite Cotehele and the River Tamar from the north

What's in a name?
Cotehele (pronounced 'coat-heel') probably means 'wood on an estuary' deriving from old Cornish *cote* for 'wood', and *hele* for 'estuary'. Today, narrow roads replace the river's tidal waters as the means of bringing goods and visitors to the estate.

Early Edgcumbes

In 1353 Hilaria de Cotehele and William Edgcumbe were young, in love and about to be married. The de Coteheles were 'old money', and above the Edgcumbes in the social hierarchy. William was the first Edgcumbe to marry an heiress, and the first to own Cotehele. It was a dynasty that was to last for nearly six centuries.

A William de Cotehele, about whom we know very little, is recorded in 1270. In 1353 his descendent Hilaria married William Edgcumbe, while still in her teens, 'declaring by petition that she would have none other'. Her older

brother Ralph was dead by 1351, possibly from the Black Death, which eradicated one third of England's population. The heroic story of William and Hilaria's great-grandson, Richard, is immortalised on a plaque in the Chapel-in-the-Wood (page 47), which he built around 1485 to give thanks for his legendary escape from Henry Trenowth of Bodrugen, agent to King Richard III, against whom he had rebelled two years earlier.

Richard Edgcumbe was the first of three generations to rebuild Cotehele between 1485 and the 1560s. The outside appearance of the house has not changed very much since that time, but inside only the Hall, Kitchen and Chapel remain relatively intact.

A second home

Cotehele's history of habitation is a complex one. Richard's grandson, Richard Edgcumbe II, built Mount Edgcumbe House in 1547–53 and went to live there, whilst his stepmother remained in residence at Cotehele as the building work continued.

The family briefly moved back to Cotehele in the mid-17th century when Colonel Piers remodelled the interior, but after his death in 1666 his son Richard returned to Mount Edgcumbe. In 1862 Cotehele's East Range was remodelled for Lady Caroline and her unmarried daughter, Ernestine, who remained in residence until the early 1900s. The World Wars took their toll and Mount Edgcumbe was destroyed by bombs in 1941, forcing Piers 5th Earl of Mount Edgcumbe to move to Cotehele, where he died in 1944.

Opposite A 19th-century painted shield showing the coat of arms of Edgcumbe impaling Cotehele

Left Mount Edgcumbe from the south-west

The men who made Cotehele

Although Cotehele was a second home for most of its post-medieval existence, the Edgcumbes never lost interest in their ancestral seat, and this sustained affection pervades the atmosphere to this day. Ironically, many visitors remark that Cotehele House feels lived in.

Early Edgcumbes built

Richard Edgcumbe I is famed for his rebellion against King Richard III (page 47). He started to modernise Cotehele House and built the Chapel-in-the-Wood, one of the romantic and memorable features of Cotehele.

His son, Piers Edgcumbe I, widened the Hall (moving the south front further into Hall Court), and installing the impressive arch-braced roof. His descendants still refer to this room as 'Piers' Hall'. He rebuilt the Chapel in the main house, and created two additional courtyards to the north and the west. His son, Richard Edgcumbe II, added the Retainers' Court buildings to the west, and the distinctive Gatehouse (south) and North-west Towers. He heightened the Hall, which involved dismantling and re-erecting the roof. He also built and relocated to Mount Edgcumbe.

Below from left to right
Richard Edgcumbe I
(1443–89)

Richard, 1st Baron
Edgcumbe (1680–1758)

George, 3rd Baron and
1st Earl of Mount
Edgcumbe (1721–95)

Colonel Piers Edgcumbe (1610–66) favoured Cotehele over Mount Edgcumbe, and moved his family back to the old house. He extensively remodelled Cotehele's interior in 1652, installing the main stairs and dividing the Great Chamber, sweeping away much of its Tudor layout.

Later Edgcumbes embellished

In the 1750s, Richard 1st Baron modernised Mount Edgcumbe, sending the old furnishings up the river to Cotehele. Whether by accident or design, antiquarian Cotehele was born, and was actively cultivated by his younger son George, grandson Richard and great-grandson Ernest. George 1st Earl further raised Cotehele's profile by hosting a royal visit in 1789, and Cotehele started to attract early tourists.

Around 1800, Richard 2nd Earl probably gave the rooms elaborate names, such as 'King Charles' and 'Queen Anne'. Cotehele was a playhouse to him. He occasionally stayed during the summer, and is said to have lived in 'Elizabethan manner'. The first guidebook,

Cothele on the Banks of the Tamar by Nicholas Condy, was published shortly after his death, and was dedicated to his son Ernest 3rd Earl.

While William modified

In 1862, William 4th Earl remodelled Cotehele's East Range as a dower house for his widowed mother, Lady Caroline. William had a deep interest in the building and in family history. He did not regard Cotehele as a shrine to Georgian antiquarianism as his ancestors had done. He shifted furnishings around to suit his own taste, evidence of which is recorded in numerous early photographs. These photographs may have been his own handiwork, as his uncle and namesake, William Henry Fox Talbot, was the famous pioneer of modern photography. William's son, Piers 5th Earl, seems to have rearranged the rooms to reflect the settings depicted by Condy.

Above from left to right
Richard, 2nd Earl of Mount Edgcumbe (1764–1839)

Ernest, 3rd Earl of Mount Edgcumbe (1797–1861)

William, 4th Earl of Mount Edgcumbe (1832–1917)

Below Piers, 5th Earl of Mount Edgcumbe (1865–1944)

Later owners

Piers 5th Earl was resident at Cotehele when he died in 1944, three years after Mount Edgcumbe House was destroyed by incendiary bombs. When his second cousin Kenelm and his wife Lilian became 6th Earl and Countess, the entire family moved to Cotehele.

For the first time in nearly three centuries the house – all of it – became a family home, albeit as a temporary measure. This was a shock for the small number of staff at Cotehele. Among the 'invaders' was Lady Hilaria (Gibbs née Edgcumbe, 1908–2009), who recalled:

'We were met by the whole staff, the housekeeper a very formidable lady … the housemaid … was holding up a huge umbrella not over me but over the housekeeper! And the housekeeper was really horrified to see us. We had children, lots of children, and they hadn't had children at Cotehele for two generations … [we] slept all over the place … the only bathroom for the children was the one in the solar behind the tapestries and they used to come trooping across the courtyard in their nighties with their little candles looking like Wee Willie Winkie!'

One of the youngest residents was Lady Hilaria's daughter Rosamund, who, in 2011, celebrated her 70th birthday at Cotehele. Her recollections of Cotehele are amongst her earliest childhood memories:

'It was a magical time for us. During the latter years of the War, with Mount Edgcumbe burnt out by an incendiary bomb, we took refuge in Cotehele.... As one of 11 grandchildren at the time, I have vivid memories of our life there.... No electricity.... Spooky nooks and crannies behind the tapestries.... The darkly cold stone steps winding up to our favourite Tower playground.... Sharing with my tiny cousins the enormous four-poster bed in the Red Room.... Tin baths…. Guttering candles.... The slippy-slidey wide wooden staircase.... Creaky floors.... Crunchy apples from an old tree in the garden.... Wonderfully damp aromas of shrubberies.... The richly warm smell of dairy cows at the gate.... Hide-and-seek in the Dungeon.... The bloodstain under the archway.... Watching Chapel services from above.... Being lifted up to look through the "spy-hole" into the Great Hall below.... Our imaginations thrived.... And, above all else, the lasting impression of love for that beautiful place.'

For safe keeping

In 1947, Cotehele passed to the National Trust in lieu of death duties through the National Land Fund. The contents remained in Edgcumbe ownership until they too were transferred in 1974.

Cotehele House

The house is a complex building, mainly formed of locally quarried slate and granite. At one time it would have been rendered, but over the years this has fallen away, revealing its hotchpotch construction.

1 Gatehouse Tower
2 South Range
3 Hall Court
4 Hall Range
5 West Range
6 Retainers' Court
7 Chapel
8 Parlour Range
9 North-west Tower
10 North Range
11 Kitchen Court
12 Butler's House
13 East Range

The main building phases at Cotehele

Tudor	1485–89	Richard Edgcumbe I
	1489–1539	Piers Edgcumbe I
	1539–62	Richard Edgcumbe II
Stuart	1652	Colonel Piers Edgcumbe
Victorian	1862	William 4th Earl

These artistic representations by Brian Byron show the possible development of the Tudor house.

Top By c.1450 the medieval house was a simple hall house with adjacent chapel and service wing within a single courtyard (Hall Court)

Above By c.1530 Piers Edgcumbe I had widened the Hall, moved the kitchens to the back of the house and created a walled garden next to the Chapel. The walls were rendered white

Right By c.1560 Richard Edgcumbe II had raised the Hall roof. It is possible that he had added the Gatehouse Tower and North-west Tower by this point. He had also built a malt house, brew house, dairy and meeting room (Retainers' Court)

Reading Cotehele

Is Cotehele an unaltered Tudor house, as is often claimed? The answer is no. As in most ancient houses, its owners made changes to suit their needs. The result is a complex building that can be difficult to decipher. The dates and purposes of its various alterations continue to challenge historians.

South Range and Gatehouse Tower

The high small windows suggest this range was built with defence in mind. It is hard to imagine how it looked before Richard Edgcumbe II built the Gatehouse Tower in the centre of it.

Hall Court

Piers Edgcumbe I widened the Hall in c.1500. The south wall (1) was brought forward, causing the Chapel (2) to appear squashed into a corner. His son Richard Edgcumbe II increased the height of the Hall, evident in the two rows of large granite blocks on top of the earlier slate-stone wall (3). He also installed the large window at the gable end of the Great Chamber (4), further dwarfing the Chapel. The ogee-headed (describing a type of arch) windows that can be seen along this wall are also found on Mount Edgcumbe House, which he built 1547–53.

West Range

The first floor of the 16th-century West Range (5) may once have provided lodgings for a resident priest or chaplain. It was formerly one big room with a timber roof and large fireplace.

Above The Hall Court, after Nicholas Condy, c.1840

Left Watercolour of the South Range, dated 1795. Artist unknown, possibly a family member (Courtesy of the Earl of Mount Edgcumbe)

North-west Tower

This was built around the 1550s. It contains the White Room with two closets (8) and the Old Drawing Room (9), and on the top floor Queen Anne's (11) and King Charles' Rooms (12) were created by partitioning one large room. It was altered in 1652, when the windows on the corner were added (10). Two small blocked-in windows (13) may be Victorian insertions to authenticate the belief that a staircase once lay behind them.

North Range

This part of the house is almost always in shadow. We know that some of the first floor rooms provided accommodation for servants in the late 1800s and early 1900s.

Left The Chapel remodelled by Piers Edgcumbe I around 1500

Below The North-west Tower and Parlour Range

Chapel

The Tudor Chapel, licensed in 1411, was completely remodelled by Piers Edgcumbe I around 1500. The bell-cote is of a style found in Brittany.

Parlour Range

The Dining Room (1) and Punch Room (2) would once have formed the parlour. Above them was the Great Chamber (solar), partitioned by Colonel Piers Edgcumbe in 1652 to form the Upper Landing (3), Red Room (4) and South Room (5), served by a latrine (6), which nowadays has an internal window (a late 18th-century embellishment) overlooking the Chapel. An open timber roof, similar to the Hall's, was sealed off as an attic (7). The buttresses were added in the 19th century, for no discernable reason.

East Range

The East Range was in a semi-derelict state before it was remodelled in 1862. You can see the changes by comparing these two photos. The extension at the north (right-hand) end was the Butler's House, built to accommodate Lady Caroline's servants.

Barn

This late medieval building was used for agricultural purposes until its conversion to a restaurant in the 1970s.

Nature notes
Cotehele's outside walls are covered with lichens. Each lichen species consists of two components – a fungus and an alga, a primitive type of plant. The mutually beneficial relationship between the fungus and alga is known as symbiosis. Lichens are very slow growing and can help to date buildings. They are only found where the air is comparatively clean.

'The deserted state of this wing was visible in the decay of the ornamented roof, & the growth of the ivy which had penetrated thro' the wall, & was hanging in festoons about the fireplace. Three or four years ago some of this ivy was removed, for fear of its pulling down the old granite chimney outside – & several pieces as thick as a man's arm were taken out by removing some of the stones. It continues to flourish nevertheless, though without any apparent root. The few rooms that were inhabited by the farming man & his wife were kept in such a dirty & wretched state, that their presence could no longer be tolerated – A small cottage was built for them in the orchard – & now the whole is at last in hand.'

Lady Caroline, 1862

Above left **The East Range**, c.1860

Above right **The East Range in 2007**

Make do and mend

Antiques have always been admired and desired. These days we tend to restore damaged antiques, but in the past it was quite common to break them up and re-display the salvaged elements as part of a new object. Several artefacts at Cotehele have been reinvented in this way.

1 Roundels containing carved heads were a common decorative feature in Tudor times. This one has been re-used as a centrepiece for an 18th-century chair in the Hall. The whole chair was covered in dark gloopy paint to make it seem like a single piece of furniture.

2 This boar's head panel is one of three sections of weaving salvaged from a late medieval or early Tudor tapestry. Two boars' heads have been incorporated into a 17th-century tapestry border in the Dining Room; a third is within a very old border, possibly part of the tapestry to which the boars' heads originally belonged.

3 This verdure tapestry (mainly green foliage) may have been commissioned for Cotehele by Piers Edgcumbe I in c.1510. The Tudor roses signified loyalty to the Crown. Regrettably, at some point in the 18th or 19th century, it was cut to fit around the door of Queen Anne's Room.

Lessons from the past

'Up-cycling', or the re-use and re-invention of discarded objects is a popular pastime today. We think of it as a new trend, but the Edgcumbes had been doing it for centuries. They were not alone – evidence of re-invention of historic objects, spanning several centuries, can be seen everywhere. Mass production and mass disposal go hand in hand, and both are relatively new. As concerns about sustainability become a feature of the modern world, we look to the customs that were second nature to our thrifty ancestors.

Tudor Cotehele (1485–1562)

Tudor Cotehele was mainly formed by three generations of the Edgcumbe family – Richard, his son Piers and his grandson Richard. They gained their wealth through political alliances and good marriages.

Richard Edgcumbe I risked his life to help Henry Tudor to become king (page 47), and Piers' first wife, Joan Durnford, brought with her a dowry of land at East and West Stonehouse (now part of Plymouth and Mount Edgcumbe respectively). Her family coat of arms displays a ram's head, which appears several times in the Hall and the Chapel. Piers' second wife, Catherine, was a wealthy widow with royal ancestry, helping Piers to climb another rung of the social ladder.

A house not a home

From 1485, when the Edgcumbes started to rebuild Cotehele, Richard Edgcumbe I was often away on royal service. Piers Edgcumbe I spent much of his time at Stonehouse. Richard Edgcumbe II built Mount Edgcumbe and went to live there before he had completed Cotehele. It therefore seems unlikely that Cotehele was ever a fully functioning and lived-in Tudor home.

This may partly explain why the Hall, the Chapel and Kitchen have largely retained their Tudor integrity and character. The rest of the house was dramatically altered by Richard Edgcumbe II's great grandson, Colonel Piers Edgcumbe, in 1652.

Above Piers Edgcumbe's armorial crest featured a stag's head whereas later Edgcumbes favoured that of a boar

Below left Heraldic stained glass in the Hall showing the arms of Edgcumbe impaling Durnford

Opposite The Hall is one of Cotehele's most distinctively Tudor rooms

Nature notes
Piers I's accounts from 1510 refer to a 'venison pastie', and in 1515, with the king's permission, he enclosed deer parks at West Stonehouse and Cotehele. A stag's head formed his armorial crest, but his father and his descendents used a boar's head or a standing boar. Although there is no longer an enclosed park at Cotehele, wild deer live in the woods. They are usually seen at twilight, the commonest type being the roe deer.

Clues to Tudor Cotehele

The Chapel, Hall and Kitchen are indicative of Cotehele's appearance in Tudor times. The 1652 building works changed the layout and character of the rest of the house, which is dominated by later additions and embellishments.

Civil War Cotehele (1640s–50s)

By the mid-1650s, for the first time in over a century, the family was living at Cotehele, Colonel Piers and Mary at its head. Smoke would have risen from the chimneys, and the house would have been filled with the sound of children's voices – Catherine, Winifred, Richard and Francis. The physical impact of their return was enormous.

1 It's possible that Cotehele's walls were clad with linenfold panelling before the 1652 alterations.

2 Pre-dating the ceiling you see today, there was an open, arch-braced roof similar to that in the Hall.

3 There is evidence of render on the external walls of the North-west Tower.

4 Before the oak stairs were installed, an enclosed, winder staircase led from beyond the north-west corner of the Hall directly into the Great Chamber. It terminated in the approximate position of today's Red Room fireplace.

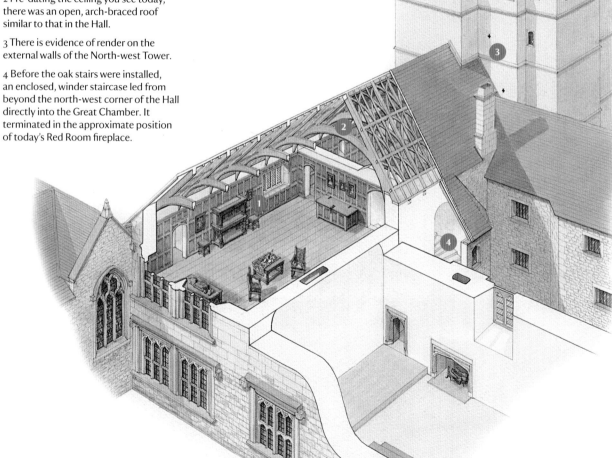

Colonel Piers was an active Royalist supporter during the Civil War, which was a risky choice as Plymouth was largely Parliamentarian. Mount Edgcumbe was damaged in 1644, and Colonel Piers was forced to surrender to the Parliamentarians. However he managed to get away with a hefty fine, keeping his estate intact. It may have been the damage to Mount Edgcumbe, the uncomfortable political climate, or personal choice that influenced Colonel Piers' decision to move his family to Cotehele. Whatever the reason, he remained at Cotehele until his death in 1666, during which time he made substantial changes to the house so it could better accommodate his and his family's needs.

5 In 1652 the open, arch-braced roof was sealed off. This now forms an attic and can be viewed on special open days.

6 In 1652 two partitions were installed in the former Great Chamber, creating three new rooms, now known as the South Room, the Red Room and the Upper Landing.

7 At some point before or after 1652, the render was removed from the exterior of the North-west Tower.

8 In 1652 the old winder staircase was removed. A solid wall replaced the former opening into the Great Chamber. A new, straight staircase was built using oak from the Cotehele estate, opening to the new Lower Landing, the latter replacing a room at the end of the North Range.

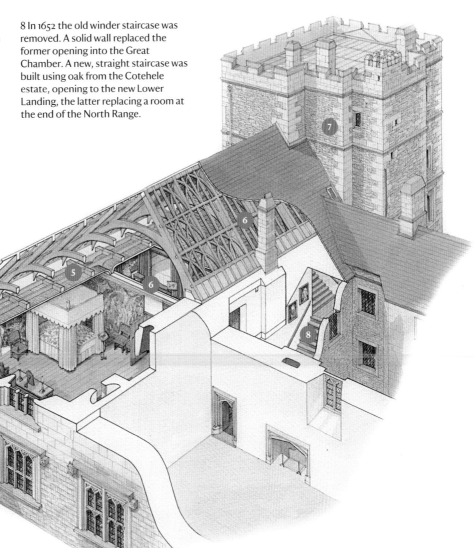

Colonel Piers' remodelling

Colonel Piers wrote and drew copious plans for the building work. In 1650 timber was being felled at Cotehele in preparation for extensive remodelling: '8 or 9 of best oaks for timber for my own use in Comfort wood, & 14 standards in wood under the way to the quay and 50–60 trees in Longwood by quay for such use as I should have for them'. The main stairs were installed by Colonel Piers, but some of the timber may have been used to make a set of simple but functional folding tables, seven of which survive at Cotehele. His plans show a significant amount of wood panelling on the walls, suggesting that the tapestries – such a defining feature of Cotehele – were introduced at a later date.

Colonel Piers' sons

In 1665, 18-year-old Francis Edgcumbe was killed in a duel he instigated after a night of drinking and brawling. Apart from the emotional impact on the family, his death-by-misadventure must have caused some embarrassment. Colonel Piers did not live to see his elder son and heir, Richard, marry the daughter of the 1st Earl of Sandwich, Anne Montagu, in 1671. They returned to live at Mount Edgcumbe. It is thought that the Red Room's impressive French bed, which would have been extremely fashionable and expensive when new, was part of Anne's wedding dowry. A treasured heirloom, it may have been moved to Cotehele by their son, Richard 1st Baron, when he remodelled Mount Edgcumbe house in the mid-18th century.

Right The Red Room bed may have come to Cotehele with the marriage of Colonel Piers' son to Anne Montagu, the daughter of the 1st Earl of Sandwich

Nature notes
The Cotehele estate is home to at least seven species of bats, including greater and lesser horseshoe, Daubenton's, brown long-eared and pipistrelle. When Colonel Piers separated off the Great Chamber roof in 1652, he created a perfect environment for bats.

Life after Colonel Piers

Colonel Piers died in 1666 and is buried in Calstock. His will states: 'I give unto my dear wife [Mary] two hundred pounds in money to be paid her within six months after my death & my will is, that during her life, she shall have the use of the household furniture at Cuttele [Cotehele] in both of the Parlors there, my own Lodging chamber, & in the room near to it, over the Larder, as also of that in the outer Dining Room, and of the upper Tower Chamber together with the utensils belonging to the Kitchen and Cellars….' Mary lived out her widowhood at Cotehele as did her daughter-in-law's mother, Jemima Montagu. Cotehele, once again, was relegated to second-home status.

Fishy business

In 1647 a whale was washed up on Edgcumbe land, near Bodrugan on the south coast of Cornwall. Colonel Piers' brother Richard described it as being 'soe odious to the smell as that I could not endure to come near itt but with taking the windy side att a pretty distance'. It is hard to believe that this stinking carcass was considered a valuable commodity. Could the jawbones in the Hall be a trophy from this unfortunate beast?

Above Richard Edgcumbe, son and heir of Colonel Piers and Mary

Georgian Cotehele (1750s–1830s)

In 1694, Richard inherited Mount Edgcumbe and Cotehele, and presided over the estates for the next 64 years. In 1742 he became 1st Baron Edgcumbe, and around that time he modernised Mount Edgcumbe house, sending the unwanted furnishings up the Tamar to be displayed in Cotehele. Thus began the tradition of presenting Cotehele to the outside world as an antiquarian house.

Richard's younger son, George 3rd Baron, inherited in 1761 and, with his wife Emma, worked hard to enhance Cotehele's romantic appeal. This included restoring the Chapel-in-the-Wood, providing a tantalising glimpse of Cotehele for approaching visitors, who invariably arrived by river.

The zenith of George and Emma's antiquarian ambitions was when King George III and Queen Charlotte visited Cotehele on 25 August 1789, during their stay at Saltram. The royal couple and entourage arrived by river but it was to be a flying visit. The king and queen, by the time they got from the quay to the house, would have had little over an hour for their tour and their breakfast combined, before having to set off again.

Above The Chapel-in-the-Wood, published in *The Beauties of England and Wales* in 1809

A royal report

Queen Charlotte's journal provides us with our first written description of Cotehele's interior. She describes the rooms by function, rather than by name. The visitor route has remained the same ever since.

'[We] landed at the woods of Cotehill ½ hour after 10 where we found Lrd & Ldy Mount Edgcumbe ready to receive Us. We went in their Coach up to this Old Family seat of theirs where His Ancestors lived at least 200 Years before they had Mount Edgcumbe. It … Consists of a large Hall full of Old Armour and Swords and Old Carved Chairs of the Times a Drawing Room hung with Old Tapestry, the Scirtingboard of which is straw and the Chair Seats made of the Priests Vestements. A Chapel which is still in good repair. The Window painted Glass but damaged and defaced. A small Bed Chamber, 2 Closets & a Dressingroom all Hung with Old Tapestry. Above stairs there is a Drawingroom The Chairs Black Ebony Carved & a Cabinet the same, & 4 Bedchambers all Hung the Same. At Breakfast we Eat off the Old Family Pewter, & used Silver knives Forks & Spoons which have been Time immemorial in the Family & have always been kept at this place…. We embarked again 10 minutes after 12.'

This quotation has been printed with the permission of Her Majesty Queen Elizabeth II.

'Breakfast'

This was the main event of the royal visit, and the most important meal the Edgcumbes were likely to host at Cotehele. It may seem odd that they served food on pewter, rather than on fine china or silver – but it was all part of the experience. The 'Old Family Pewter', by virtue of its age and association with Cotehele (the coat of arms of the Edgcumbe ancestors are engraved on the rims) seems to have impressed the queen and was deemed fit for the king. Custom has it that they dined in the Old Drawing Room, but this cannot be proved.

Above Pewter mugs and plates on the refectory table in the Hall

Left Queen Charlotte, after Allan Ramsay

A royal tour

accounts for their subsequent removal. The chair seats mentioned are no longer at Cotehele, but typify the culture of re-invention that applies to many objects in the house.

'The Desert Plates are Old Delph of a very large Size but make no part of the Old Family Furniture'
These plates are displayed on the table in the centre of the Dining Room. The queen's observation that they were not part of the 'old family furniture' shows how important the link between family, object and historic location was considered to be.

Chapel
'A Chapel which is still in good repair. The Window painted Glass but damaged and defaced'
The east window was restored in 1888, a century after the royal visit.

Punch and White Rooms
'A small Bed Chamber, 2 Closets & a Dressingroom all Hung with Old Tapestry'
Two closets are concealed behind the tapestry in the White Room. It seems that the Punch Room was, at that time, the dressing room mentioned by the queen.

Left The Hall, after Nicholas Condy, c.1840

Below The Delft bottles admired by Queen Charlotte

Hall
'a large Hall full of Old Armour and Swords and Old Carved Chairs of the Times'

Dining Room
'a Drawing Room hung with Old Tapestry, the Scirtingboard of which is straw and the Chair Seats made of the Priests Vestements'
It's interesting that the Dining Room is referred to as a 'Drawing Room'. The 'scirtingboard of straw' refers to dado panels, woven from rush or grasses. They would have been damp, and a haven for pests, which

Red, South, King Charles' and Queen Anne's Rooms
'& 4 Bedchambers all Hung the Same'
This refers to the Red, South, King Charles' and Queen Anne's Rooms. The lack of detail may suggest that the visit was rather hurried owing to the receding tide. Or it could mean that these rooms were considered of insufficient interest to explore in detail. It's reasonable to infer from this description that these four rooms were hung with tapestry.

Old Drawing Room
'Above stairs there is a Drawingroom The Chairs Black Ebony Carved & a Cabinet the same'
The cabinet referred to is not ebony, but had been coated in black paint to make it match the other furnishings. On the ebony settee two cushions bearing the names 'King George' and 'Queen Charlotte' can be found, but the royal couple did not sit here. They had individual chairs (no longer at Cotehele), which were afterwards furnished with commemorative brass plaques. These were later removed because too many visitors sat on the chairs, causing damage.

'The Decanters are of the year 1646 the name of the Wines burnt in the Earthenware for that Time Wines were sold at the Apothecaries Shop & in Sending such a Decanter it was filled with the Wine it bore the Label off'
The queen's description of the decanters is romantic but impractical. It would be nonsensical to have a servant travel to the nearest apothecary to refill such small vessels. Even quite modest households would keep a store of wine at that time, and many would make their own. However, Queen Charlotte was not alone in her naïvety; many Georgian and Victorian visitors shared a ready belief in the stories that grew up around Cotehele, sustained by its antiquarian charm and beguiling atmosphere.

Above left The Old Drawing Room, after Nicholas Condy, c.1840

Above right King Charles' Room, after Nicholas Condy, c.1840

Victorian Cotehele (1837–1901)

In the 19th century, perhaps as an indirect result of industrialisation, people became increasingly nostalgic about the past. Cotehele was an embodiment of the 'good old days' and became a popular destination for early tourists.

George and Emma's grandson, Ernest 3rd Earl died in 1861. His son William continued to live at Mount Edgcumbe and remodelled Cotehele's East Range as a home for his mother and sister. In 1862, Lady Caroline and Ernestine moved to live at Cotehele. A door, now blocked, opened from Caroline and Ernestine's Breakfast Room into the old Hall, signifying the boundary between two worlds. Behind it, mother and daughter lived their everyday lives. Beyond it

Cotehele Court Dinner
This painting was a gift from the 'tenantry of Mount Edgcumbe' to Deeble Boger, the land agent. The event was described by the 4th Earl: 'ample justice was done to the roast beef and plum pudding (eaten together as was the custom) … and, the Rector having said Grace, the singers having taken their places at the bottom of the Hall … the hot punch ladled out; the time-honoured toasts had been duly honoured … the tenants had all gradually retired and ridden off by moonlight down the steep hill – some of them with a jovial recklessness to the risk of their necks….'
(Courtesy of Mount Edgcumbe House.)

Above The south elevation romantically depicted in *Cothele on the Banks of the Tamar*

Right The title page from Nicholas Condy's book showing figures in 17th-century dress

Opposite Trestle tables in the Hall set for tea, late 19th century

stood the ancient part of the house, around which privileged visitors would tiptoe with reverence and awe. The old house's status was enshrined in the servants' rules: 'No Man Servant to enter the kitchen or any part of the Old House except the Footman or any Servant in Waiting on the Parlour.'

Cotehele's first guidebook

Throughout the 19th century visitors were encouraged to come and see the old house, and by the time Lady Caroline and Ernestine took up residence, the book *Cotehele on the Banks of the Tamar* had been in circulation for over two decades, with coloured prints of the showrooms and descriptions extolling its ancient virtues. Lady Caroline was well acquainted with its creator, Plymouth artist Nicholas Condy. His book was more about pictures than words, which were added by the Reverend Arundell of nearby Landulph Church.

Lady Caroline's correspondence

Lady Caroline dedicated much of her time to writing letters. Hundreds of letters to her brother, William Henry Fox Talbot of Lacock Abbey (Lady Caroline's childhood home), survive and provide a charming insight into her character. In 1862, following her arrival at Cotehele, she instructed William (whom she called Henry) on the art of addressing letters: 'Don't omit *House* – as otherwise the letters go to Cotehele Quay – by Callington – & don't put Cornwall, because Tavistock is *Devon* tho' Cotehele is not. So put no county.'

Fox Talbot was the pioneer of modern photography, a hobby that was enthusiastically taken up at Cotehele – at one point the little annex to the Library was used as a dark room.

Entertainment at Cotehele

Lady Ernestine's handwritten and lovingly annotated manuscript book was recently purchased for Cotehele. It includes compositions by her mother, her grandfather, and even a piece 'copied from Uncle George's music book, and sung by him', as well as some popular classics, such as 'Trelawny' (two compositions), and 'O the Roast Beef of Old England'. There are lots of hymns and political and patriotic songs such as 'My Maryland – Confederate song' amongst others. Lady Ernestine may well have played on the reed organ in the Victorian Library, which has recently been restored to playing order for visitors to enjoy.

'I do not propose to keep this Journal as a regular daily account of my life & occupations. It seems to me mere waste of time to record day after day "went out walking in the morning & riding in the afternoon: saw no one: played on the piano, wrote letters & read the papers" and when my Mother & I are living here alone there would be little else to say.'

Lady Ernestine's 1871 journal

Make do and mend

Re-use of old carvings became very fashionable in the Victorian era. In 1864 Lady Caroline wrote: 'I intend going to Exeter tomorrow with a return ticket, to look for some old carving for Cotehele.' This Victorian photo shows ceramics displayed on a sideboard made from old carvings. The sideboard can be seen in the Victorian Breakfast Room at Cotehele. Similarly, the cupboard under the stairs in the Victorian Library incorporates old pieces of oak carved furniture and mouldings.

In 1881, during a visit to Saltram, Lady Caroline was taken ill and later died. Lady Ernestine continued to live at Cotehele until about 1905, and was looked after by the butler and housekeeper, Mr and Mrs Paddon, and their staff.

Left Lady Caroline (1808–81) (Courtesy of the Earl of Mount Edgcumbe)

Above Lady Ernestine (1843–1925) (Courtesy of the Earl of Mount Edgcumbe)

Twentieth-century Cotehele

The late 19th and early 20th century at Cotehele was dominated by Lady Ernestine. Her brother, William 4th Earl, employed a butler, housekeeper and a team of servants to look after her needs.

John Paddon was the butler. He married Alice née Chaffey, who was in service at Cotehele as a cook when they married in 1881. She later became housekeeper. They lived in the Butler's House, and were still in residence in 1911 according to the census. They had four children, three boys and a girl.

Tragedy struck the Paddons when their daughter Alice died after breaking her ankle. Her wound became infected and her leg was amputated, but it was too late. She is buried in Calstock churchyard. Around 1905, Lady Ernestine moved out of Cotehele to nearby Honeycombe Manor (now a holiday park). She died in 1925. In her will, she left £50 to Alice Paddon.

'Lord of a Lordly House'

In 1906, widower William, 4th Earl married his recently widowed cousin, Caroline Cecilia, Countess of Ravensworth. They were 74 and 67 years old respectively.

William often stayed in the Old Drawing Room and Caroline in the South Room (then the 'Best Bedroom'). In 1909, a few days after her 70th birthday, Caroline died of a fever. Their brief marriage is commemorated in a plaque in the Chapel.

The end of an era

William died in 1917. His son Piers 5th Earl and his wife Edith spent a lot of time at Cotehele. They were good landlords, and a few long-standing tenants still remember 'Lordy' with fondness.

In 1940, the 5th Earl must have been devastated when his 26-year-old heir presumptive, Piers Richard (his second cousin once removed), was killed in action near Dunkirk. The following year Mount Edgcumbe House was destroyed by incendiary bombs. Piers Richard's sister, Hilaria, recalled: 'The fire was so horrific and so hot that the silver ran from the silver safe in a molten stream'.

This marked the end of an era for the Edgcumbes of Cotehele and Mount Edgcumbe. Piers died in 1944. In the wake of two World Wars, Cotehele's future was hanging in the balance.

Make do and mend

Queen Mary visited Cotehele in 1938. She took a great interest in this sword. It was at one time thought to have belonged to the Black Prince (Edward, Prince of Wales, son of Edward III). However, this is impossible. The sword is a composite, with an early 17th-century German blade, a (possibly) Scottish guard and the handle topped with a pommel from yet another object. The earliest part is 250 years too late for its alleged provenance.

The Bystander, August 19, 1908   377

Lord of a Lordly House

THE EARL AND COUNTESS OF MOUNT EDGCUMBE AT COTEHELE, CORNWALL

Photo]   AN INTERESTING GROUP AT THE FINE MAIN DOORWAY   *[Leonard Willoughby*

The Earl and Countess of Mount Edgcumbe with a favourite dog, Pepper, at the doorway of their mediæval home, which came to the family about the year 1353, when Hilaria of Cotehele married an Edgcumbe of Edgcumbe. Cotehele House is one of the finest examples of mediæval domestic architecture in the country, and a place of many interesting memories, as well as a treasure-house of beautiful things. The Earl is Lord-Lieutenant of the County of Cornwall. (Other illustrations on pages 389-392)

Above William, 4th Earl of Mount Edgcumbe and his new wife Caroline

New beginnings

Kenelm and Lilian, second cousins to Piers 5th Earl, inherited in 1944. Kenelm was 71. His daughter Hilaria said he had been landed with a 'smoking ruin' and an 'antique manor house'. He decided to rebuild Mount Edgcumbe and to give Cotehele to the National Trust.

In 1946, James Lees-Milne, famed diarist and author, was working as Country Houses Secretary for the National Trust. His memoirs record his stay at Cotehele during negotiations with the 6th Earl: 'I am given the bedroom at the top of the entrance gate-tower, approached by a twisting stone staircase, and in isolation … lightning during the night … flashed through my casements and lit up the great tower and the courtyard.' The following day, having 'slept ill', he was incredulous when: '[Lady Mount Edgcumbe's] Cairn puppy ate a good slice of Queen Anne's tatting from the famous needlework sofa in the Punch Room. "You naughty little thing," she admonished in an amused tone as it scuttled off with a mouthful.'

Fortunately, discussions didn't similarly unravel. Negotiations were successful, and Kenelm and Lilian were able to announce their plans to anxious tenants.

Above Kenelm 6th Earl in front of the ruins of Mount Edgcumbe (Courtesy of the Earl of Mount Edgcumbe)

Left James Lees-Milne as Country Houses Secretary for the National Trust

A memorable gift

In 1947 Cotehele was transferred to the National Trust via the Treasury in lieu of death duties, through the National Land Fund. Kenelm and Lilian considered it to be a war memorial in remembrance of their dead son, Piers Richard.

During a dedication service in Cotehele Chapel in 1981, the National Trust's Michael Trinick said: 'We hold the estate as a memorial to the 300,000 men and women who fell in the last war. In remembering them we remember in particular Piers Edgcumbe. His sword, hanging in the home of his ancestors, gives visible expression to the trust which his parents reposed in us.'

Following Kenelm 6th Earl's death in 1965, his cousin Edward, from New Zealand, became the 7th Earl. His nephew, Robert, is the 8th and current Earl. He divides his time between his native New Zealand and a cottage near his ancestral home on the Mount Edgcumbe estate.

Above The 6th Earl and Countess (with her Cairn terrier) explaining to tenants that the National Trust will be their new landlord

Below Piers' memorial and sword in Cotehele Chapel

The yuletide tradition of decking the Tudor Hall with a garland is a relatively recent one, begun in the 1950s. It is now firmly established as one of Cotehele's annual highlights.

What's in the garland?

The exact selection of flowers varies each year depending on the weather and other variables. However, they usually include …

statice for blues and purples

helipterum, for white

helichrysum, such as the 'Dargan Hill Monarch', for gold

Limonium suworowii or 'pink pokers', for pink

The making of the garland

The flowers that decorate the garland are grown in Cotehele's Cut Flower Garden. The seeds are sown in February, and cut daily in the summer. Each individual stem is stripped of leaves before being bunched and hung in the potting shed to dry.

Construction begins in early November. The core of the garland is an 18-metre (60-foot) long rope of 12-millimetre diameter. The first stage is undertaken at ground level, tying bunches of pittosporum (an evergreen shrub) to the rope. This takes about a day. The green garland is then hoisted up, and attached to a fixing at each end of the Hall and to the chandelier rods to enable it to hang in swags.

When this is done, sets of flowers are put aside for each section of the garland. The final stage is for the 15–30,000 flowers to be placed individually amongst the greenery. The staff and volunteer time involved in making the garland, from conception to completion, equates to one full-time employee per year.

Witnesses to the tradition

The National Trust's Michael Trinick (1) started the tradition in the 1950s. Marie Martin née Langsford (2) was born in 1914, the daughter of Harold Langsford of Cotehele Mill, where she grew up (see page 51). She married Douglas (3) in 1942 and they had three daughters – Virginia (4), Sally (5) and Mary (6). Virginia is a writer and Mary is an artist, and both continue their close association with Cotehele (see page 63). Colonel and Mrs Julyan (7 and 8) were tenants in the East Range from *c.*1950–95. Mrs Julyan was also an artist – her studio was in the tower room (in which James Lees-Milne 'slept ill') – and Colonel Julyan was a retired teacher and academic. His subjects were farming and rural antiquities, which he called 'bygones'.

Right A carol service under the garland late 1950s (Courtesy of Mary Martin)

The Garden and Estate

The 1,300-acre riverside estate encompasses dense woodland and open fields, flora and fauna, industrial ruins and working farm buildings. No less diverse are Cotehele's gardens, surrounding the house on all sides.

Today's garden is an ever-changing canvas, evolving under the care of the garden team and advisers. New schemes are considered for their suitability for the climate and landscape, and for their colour and seasonality. The spring brings with it a glorious display of around 120 varieties of daffodil, many of them local to the Tamar Valley.

The garden

Cotehele's garden is relatively young in historical terms. There is the suggestion of a medieval or Tudor terraced garden to the north of the house, and there may once have been a walled garden in the area now occupied by Retainers' Court. Further research is required.

There was no garden to speak of when Lady Countess Caroline moved to Cotehele in 1862, and the Terraces were in a state of neglect.

Early paintings suggest the land immediately surrounding the house had been put to agricultural use, and appears to have been grazed by livestock. Lady Caroline's love of plants and flowers changed Cotehele forever.

Through two World Wars Cotehele's garden grew out of control. In the late 1940s and 1950s large areas were cleared, and many unwieldy plants were removed without trace. We are fortunate that Lady Caroline's letters provide us with an insight into how her garden grew.

1 The Terraces
2 The Bowling Green
3 The Valley Garden
4 Nelson's Piece
5 The Acer Grove
6 The Meadow
7 The Upper Garden
8 The Cut Flower Garden
9 Mrs Julyan's Garden
10 Prospect Field
11 The Old Orchard
12 The Mother Orchard

Opposite The view from the garden over the valley to Calstock and the viaduct

The Terraces

This may have been the first area to be developed by Lady Caroline. In 1872 she wrote about this area of the garden: 'Cotehele is in *perfection* just now – the Roses have been beautiful – particularly the Devoniensis & Céline Forestier –, both of the Tea kind, & deliciously sweet. The latter a lovely pale yellow – & more refined looking than the Gloire de Dijon – and the Italian jessamine [jasmine] under Ernestine's window, is the most beautiful thing I ever saw. It is something like the common jessamine – only the blossoms are a good deal larger, as well as the leaves – & it flowers in much greater profusion. The perfume too is quite delicious, & comes in at the windows. I have also two nice Orange trees in tubs, covered with fruit – about 4 or 5 foot high – They are put out among the geraniums & roses – & look exceedingly well.'

Above The Terraces in front of the East Range

Nelson's Piece

From the early 1900s, a strip of land to the north of the Valley Garden was let to Peter Nilsson, a seaman from Sweden who settled in Calstock. His family were involved in salmon fishing and market gardening, and changed their name to Nelson. Although it was transferred to the National Trust in 1955, this area is still known as Nelson's Piece.

The Acer Grove

This area in the north-east corner of the garden is planted with Japanese maples with colourful foliage in spring and autumn.

The Bowling Green

The gaming tradition continues in this area, but bowls have been replaced by croquet. The east side is fringed by young sycamore trees – the second generation of this planting scheme, around which are clustered cyclamen and autumn crocuses.

The Valley Garden

In medieval and Tudor times, the Valley Garden was a very important area. The stewpond and the dovecote provided fish and fowl for the house, and water was drawn from the wells.

When the National Trust took over in 1947, the Valley Garden was completely overgrown. Cornwall's warm, wet climate means that plants grow quickly, and a cultivated landscape, if left untended, can appear completely wild within a few years, or in some cases, months. The Valley Garden is extremely difficult to maintain. The steep slopes make it inaccessible to machinery, so everything must be carried in and out by hand. Low-maintenance shrubs formed a major element of the 1950s planting, such as the 'Cornish Red' rhododendron. Found in most gardens in Cornwall it is also popular in Devon, where it is known as 'Devon Pink'. Ferns and gunnera (giant rhubarb) are also suited to the shade of the Valley Garden. The medieval dovecote was restored in 1962, and the Victorian summerhouse was rebuilt in 1990.

Above right The East Range and Terraces painted by William Henry, 4th Earl of Mount Edgcumbe, dated 1915

Right The garden is ever-changing: *Tulip virichie* flowering on the Terraces in spring 2012

The Meadow

Spring is the best time to visit the meadow, when you can see the daffodils in their full glory. After they have passed, the grass is not cut until July to encourage wild flowers to seed. Cotehele's daffodils include Lent lily and pheasant's-eye narcissus.

Nature notes
Cotehele's daffodils in spring are a crowning glory. The late-flowering Tamar Double White is indigenous to the valley and comes out in May. It is known to have been flowering here as early as 1629.

Below Hosts of daffodils
in the Meadow

The Upper Garden

The lily pond may have been dug as late as the early 20th century. A little bridge once enabled access to the island.

At the edges of the garden, the deep borders are colour themed. The top (north) border is in 'hot' colours, and the west border is in golds and silvers, following a plan introduced by gardens adviser Graham Stuart Thomas in the 1960s.

The Cut Flower Garden

This is where flowers are grown for the house and for the garland (page 34). Nearby a greenhouse replaces the Victorian one. In September 1863, Lady Caroline wrote enthusiastically of her plan for a 'grand hothouse … to be divided in two – one for grapes, quite hot – the other cooler, for late grapes & flowers … 60 ft long. Is not that a grand idea?'

Mrs Julyan's Garden

This area is named after the tenant who cared for it from the 1950s until 1995. Today, it is planted to reflect horticulture in the Tamar Valley.

The Prospect Tower

This distinctive three-sided tower lends its name to the field in which it stands. It is something of a mystery, probably built in the mid-18th century, but no-one is certain of its intended purpose. The stairs were installed by the National Trust around 1980 to give visitors access to the surrounding views. An almost identical tower folly stood on Penlee Point on the Mount Edgcumbe estate, but was demolished in 1914.

Above The Prospect Tower

Left The lily pond in the Upper Garden in 2004

The orchards

For centuries, apple and cherry orchards have been a feature of the Tamar Valley. Many of the apples were used for making cider, a tradition that has been revived at Cotehele. The old cider press from Bovey Tracey has been installed in the Mother Orchard and is once again in working order.

The Old Orchard

A makeshift tennis court seems to have occupied the dip in the centre of the Old Orchard in the 1920s and 1930s, but has now been planted with apple trees. In November 1873, Lady Caroline wrote: 'I am, as usual, very busy in my garden and farm, which I am happy to say is very productive in apples this year – I believe there will be 25 Hogsheads [432 pints] of cider! They are very busy making it now. First pounding, then squatting.'

Nature notes

The apple lace bug is an endangered insect found in traditional apple orchards, which are themselves becoming endangered. In the UK it is exclusively found in Devon and Cornwall, where it is known to inhabit five sites, including a small orchard on the Cotehele estate, and also in the New Forest in Hampshire, where it lives in crab apple trees.

The Mother Orchard

The Mother Orchard was inspired and informed by apple collectors and propagators James Evans and Mary Martin. It was established principally to secure the future of local varieties of apple that would otherwise be threatened with extinction.

Three hundred apple trees were planted in 2007–08. Many were sponsored by members of the public, whose dedications are recorded in a donations book. The first fruit appears six years after planting. A fully grown apple tree will produce enough apples to make between 50 and 150 pints of cider.

Nature notes

The West Country custom of wassailing apple trees takes place at Cotehele around the time of the winter solstice. It involves a musical procession of people dressed in colourful clothing adorned with twigs and leaves, dancing, playing instruments, blowing whistles, ringing bells and shaking rattles. The more noise that is made, the greater the chance of driving away evil spirits who might hamper the harvest. To summon the help of good spirits, cider-soaked crusts of bread are hung in trees for the robin, who represents the tree spirit. Wassail itself is a hot alcoholic drink made with apples and spices. Two 18th-century wassail bowls can be found in Cotehele's Punch Room.

Amongst the local cultivars planted in the Mother Orchard is the Colloggett Pippin (pronounced 'cloggett'), probably originating from Colloggett Farm near Botus Fleming, a few miles from Cotehele, and Snell's White or Glass Apple. Both varieties were located by James and Mary in 1980.

Above The Old Orchard, where local varieties of apple are grown – here 'Cotehele Beauty'

Nature notes

Mistletoe, a parasitic plant that lives off the nutrients of its host plant, abounds in apple tress. Superstitions that surround it include the belief that kissing under it brings good luck, and that bringing it into a church will carry a curse.

The woodland

The densely wooded riverbanks provide the setting for a very old story that has enhanced Cotehele's dreamy atmosphere for centuries. It concerns the escape of Richard Edgcumbe I – a defining moment in Cotehele's history.

In 1483, Richard Edgcumbe I made a bold decision: to rebel against King Richard III, possibly in reaction to rumours that the king had killed his nephews and heirs to the throne – the Princes in the Tower. Henry Trenowth of Bodrugen, the king's agent, placed Edgcumbe under house arrest but he escaped by killing a sentry. The story goes that Richard made his way towards the river, taking cover in the woods and, on reaching the water's edge, placed a stone in his cap and threw it in. The king's men, in hot pursuit, heard the splash, and seeing the cap floating downstream presumed Edgcumbe had drowned. Instead, he had escaped to Brittany, and went on to fight with Henry Tudor – later King Henry VII – at the Battle of Bosworth, where he was knighted and made Comptroller of the Royal Household.

The Chapel-in-the-Wood

To commemorate his escape, Richard built the Chapel-in-the-Wood, dedicated to saints George and Thomas à Beckett. It was restored in 1769 by George 3rd Baron Edgcumbe, who had the legendary story of his ancestor inscribed on a plaque. He also commissioned a picture of the memorial from Richard Edgcumbe's tomb in Morlaix, Brittany. The copy of the memorial is in Cotehele House, and the tomb was completely destroyed during the French Revolution, which began in 1789.

Opposite top The Chapel-in-the-Wood

Opposite left The Chapel-in-the-Wood, after Nicholas Condy

Right The plaque inscribed with the story of Richard Edgcumbe's escape

Nature notes
All three species of British woodpecker are found at Cotehele. A tapestry in the house depicts the story of King Picus, with whom the sorceress Circe (pronounced Ser-see) falls in love. But Picus is in love with his wife, Canens, and rejects Circe's advances. Deeply offended, she turns him into a woodpecker. The Latin name for woodpecker is Picus. Pictured is a green woodpecker (Picus viridis)

The Great Blizzard of 1891

Richard's Chapel-in-the-Wood was fortunate to survive a terrible storm that devastated the South West in 1891. At Cotehele, thousands of trees were lost, including elm, ash, beech, sycamore, oak and Spanish (sweet) chestnuts.

The *Western Morning News* published an account of the event written by William Coulter, the 'highly respected house steward of the Earl of Mount Edgcumbe' at Cotehele, who had experienced the wrath of the storm first-hand: 'the devastation in the woods is beyond all description…. The beautiful walk from Cotehele Quay to the house is a wreck that 50 years will not set in the same form as it existed before the 9th of March…. The noise of the storm resembled the frantic yells and fiendish laughter of millions of liberated maniacs, broken, at frequent intervals,

by what sounded like deafening and rapid volleys of heavy artillery…. The appearance of the courtyard, or quadrangle, presented that of a grave-yard, the slates in all shapes, sizes, and forms, standing on end, like grave-stones projecting above the snow.'

Above Cotehele viewed from Calstock

Nature notes

Sweet chestnuts were more commonly called Spanish chestnuts in the 19th century. This enormous tree, drawn by an unknown artist in 1847 and inscribed '26ft 6 ins circumference. Contains 700 feet of timber', can no longer be found at Cotehele. It was probably lost in the Great Blizzard.

A Cotehele herbal

When we are unwell, we go to see a doctor. But in the past, people relied on plants to cure their ills, and were guided by a book called a herbal. The Edgcumbes once owned *The Grete Herball. Illust. Very old and curious. 1550.* Here are some plants found at Cotehele, with descriptions from *Culpeper's Herbal* of 1683.

1 Dandelion
'Vulgarly called *piss-a-beds*.... It wonderfully opens the passages of urine, both in young and old... The French and Dutch so often eat them in the spring ... foreign physicians are more liberal in communicating their knowledge of the virtues of plants than the English.'

2 Nettle
'... the juice of nettles, used as a gargle, allays the swelling of the almonds of the throat ... the seed ... kills worms in children; eases the spleen occasioned by wind....'

3 Foxglove
'The decoction made with sugar or honey, is effectual in cleansing and purging the body, both upwards and downwards, of tough phlegm and clammy humours, and to open obstructions of the liver and spleen.... It is a sovereign remedy for a sore head.' **Very poisonous**. Do not ingest despite Culpeper's advice!

4 Chestnut, sweet or Spanish
'... dry chestnuts, and beat the kernels into powder, both the barks being taken away, and make it up into an electuary with honey, so you have an admirable remedy for the cough and spitting blood.'

Mill memories

Marie Martin was the daughter of Harold Langsford, the miller. As children, Marie and her siblings would play on the sack hoist, which was a pulley system to raise and lower sacks of grain and flour between floors. Cats were (and still are) a familiar sight, working pets, keeping the rats at bay.

Marie Martin's daughter, Virginia Spiers, captured life at the mill in her 'Tamar Valley Diaries' for the *Guardian* newspaper in 1996.

'Eighty years ago my grandfather took over the mill after his father and grandfather, tenants of Lord Mount Edgcumbe of Cotehele. The waterwheel was geared for grinding corn, generating electricity, sawing wood for gates, making punnets and chip baskets for local fruit growers and there was a resident baker. Imported grain, bought at Plymouth's corn exchange, came upriver in the barge *Myrtle* to be unloaded into wagons and carted from Cotehele Quay. Grandfather biked up and down the valley between Murden [sic] and Glamorgan Mill, a mile upstream, supervising and patrolling ponds, sluices, leats and the wooden launders carrying water to the overshot wheels. Millstones were regularly pecked and dressed and Mr Goard, millwright of St Germans, occasionally stayed for a week, servicing the machinery and fitting new cogs cut from holly and apple wood.'

Cotehele (or Morden) Mill has existed since medieval times. From the 1870s, for almost a century, it was run by the Langsford family, after which it was restored by the National Trust and opened to visitors as a working watermill in 1973. It was restored again in 2001 and continues to produce flour for use in the restaurant and for commercial distribution.

Above Cotehele Mill, c.1970

Left Cotehele Mill's waterwheel

The mill is fed by the Morden stream, a tributary of the River Tamar. A man-made weir and a sluice gate control the flow of water into the leat, which carries the water to the 'overshot' wheel (fed from above). The leat also feeds water to the modern hydroelectric turbine.

Nature notes

In late spring and early summer the meadow between the mill and the stream is carpeted with beautiful marsh orchids. The last count was about 125.

The workshops

The National Trust created four workshops in the early 1970s to reflect rural trades of the 19th century. Their original use was mainly agricultural. The Saddler's (formerly a hayloft), Blacksmith's and Wheelwright's (formerly stables) are furnished with equipment donated by or acquired from local sources. The 1970s Carpenter's Workshop has since been converted to a studio for a local potter, and part of the Old Cherry Store is occupied by a green woodworker.

Left The Mill across the meadow

Below The Wheelwright's Workshop

Above Peter Hambly's cart

Right The Langsford family's horse and cart

The Cart Shed

The Cart Shed accommodates two locally made wagons. One was commissioned by local farmer Peter Hambly and is painted with his name. It was made by Richard Striplin from St Dominick, whose family made wheels, furniture, cherry-picker ladders – and coffins, which earned Richard the nickname 'Dicky Box'.

The Bakery

From 1898 to 1915 the building adjacent to the mill was used as a bakery. In the early 1970s, when the National Trust first opened the mill complex to visitors, a cider press was installed here. The custodian was instructed to pour scrumpy on the floor to create a suitable atmosphere. The cider press is now in Cotehele's Mother Orchard, and the bakery has been restored. Volunteers use the mill's own flour to follow a variety of recipes, including one for bread devised by Lady Hilaria, daughter of Cotehele's donor, Kenelm, 6th Earl of Mount Edgcumbe.

The Langsford family's horse and cart would have been a familiar sight to Ruth Milton (née Rogers), who spent her childhood at the quay. She remembered with fondness one particular shire horse: '[Colonel] was a useful animal, fetching, carrying corn, apples and cherries … when his work was done and he was taken over to the mill door to be relieved of the wagon and harness etc. he always trotted over to the kitchen door of the house to get his saffron cake, with his frame filling the entire doorway.'

Bound by a River

The tranquillity of the River Tamar belies its past as a trade highway. Nothing now remains of the valley's industrial past except ruined mine workings and neglected quays. Of the hundreds of merchant vessels which once plied the River Tamar, only one still sails.

Shamrock

Shamrock was built in 1899 by Frederick Hawke of Stonehouse, Plymouth. Her purpose was to carry manure, fertiliser, coal, bricks, sand and stone between the quays and harbours of Cornwall's coast and rivers.

In 1962 she became a prospecting vessel, drilling for core samples on the seabed within St Ives Bay, and was a familiar sight along the coast between Land's End and Falmouth, where she was eventually detained by the harbour master for being unseaworthy.

Fred, a former crew-member, bought her but was only permitted to take her out of the harbour under tow. Due to unexpected and appalling weather conditions, the other vessel deserted her and headed for safety, leaving Fred to take his chances with _Shamrock_ and the storm. It is a minor miracle that they made it to Plymouth Sound.

Boats are traditionally divided into 64 shares, and in 1974 the National Maritime Museum and the National Trust bought 30 and 34 shares of _Shamrock_ respectively. She underwent extensive repairs at Cotehele Quay and was fit to sail again in 1982.

Above _Shamrock_ in Plymouth Sound

Below The restored Tamar sailing barge _Shamrock_ moored alongside Cotehele Quay

Left Cotehele Quay

Cotehele Quay

In the 19th century, as local industries boomed, Cotehele Quay bustled with vessels loading and unloading cargo. Crowded paddle steamers travelled upriver from Plymouth to see the blossoming orchards for which the area was famed, and small boats carried market-gardening produce for sale at Devonport Market.

Discovery Centre

In the early 1900s, the Discovery Centre at the quay was known as Captain Bill's Store. *Myrtle* was once a familiar sight at Cotehele Quay. Skippered by Bill Martin (Captain Bill), the main commodity she carried was grain for Cotehele Mill. Sadly, she was commandeered in the Second World War and blown up during the Plymouth Blitz. A model of *Myrtle* is displayed in the Discovery Centre, as is a scale model of Goss's boatyard. James Goss rented the yard – located on the Devon bank, opposite Calstock – from the 4th Earl. The abundance of timber following the Great Blizzard of 1891 enabled Goss to build new boats, as well as maintaining existing vessels.

The Edgcumbe Tea-room

The former Edgcumbe Arms inn, frequented by Cotehele's workers and tenants, was established by 1832 and seems to have ceased trading by 1873. The sign depicts the Edgcumbe family's coat of arms.

Nature notes

Triangular club rush is a plant that is nearly extinct in the UK, but it can be found growing on the banks of a tributary of the River Tamar at Cotehele. The Environment Agency has created a special site where the plant can be nurtured away from the storms and other risks it faces along the main estuary.

Above Cotehele Quay showing Captain Bill's Store, now the Discovery Centre

Opposite The royal barge rowing ashore from the *Fairy* to land at Cotehele Quay, by Nicholas Condy, c.1846

A repeat royal visit

Queen Victoria landed twice at Cotehele Quay and it is rumoured locally that one of the cottages was built specially for Her Majesty's personal convenience.

She first visited on 21 August 1846.

'A little further on we came to Cotele [sic], with a picturesque small village & landing place. The river is very narrow here. We landed & drove up a steep hill, under the fir trees, to the very curious old house of Cotele, where we got out…. The old rooms are hung with arras [tapestry], & very cheerless, I think. We drove down another way, under beautiful trees & re-embarked, proceeding down the river.'

And again on 13 August 1856:

'Steamed up the Tamar…. At Cothele [sic] …. we took a little river steamer (a dirty little thing) to go higher up the river … [went back] on board the 'Fairy' some way below Cotele [sic], the tide having become much lower.'

These quotations have been printed with the permission of Her Majesty Queen Elizabeth II.

Market gardening

Market gardening used to be a major industry of the Tamar Valley, supported by numerous other industries. Lime burners, chip-basket (fruit-punnet) makers, dock-dung gatherers and market boat skippers all depended heavily on the fruit and flower growers for their livelihoods.

Cotehele's market gardeners grew, amongst other things, daffodils, apples and soft fruit, particularly cherries and strawberries. Local horticulturalist James Lawry visited London in 1863 and was surprised that there were no strawberries on sale in Covent Garden; after all, the railway was extended to Plymouth in 1849. The subsequent growth in the Tamar Valley market-gardening industry owes much to him, but the real boom came when the Plymouth railway was extended to Bere Alston in 1890. In his book *Industrial Archaeology of the Tamar Valley*, Frank Booker explains: 'The heavily laden and scented strawberry wagons which had previously plodded to Saltash were now diverted to Cotehele Quay, the packed fruit being ferried over the river for 1d a box to be met by the railway's vans on the Devon side. From here it went to Bere Alston station over the Earl of Mount Edgcumbe's private drive, his lordship turning a benevolent eye on traffic which bolstered his dividends.' The viaduct was built in 1908, extending the railway to Calstock, which damaged the river trade.

The market-gardening tradition continues in this area, and local growers often sell their wares at roadside for the benefit of passers-by who deposit their payment in an honesty box.

Nature notes
'Dock dung' (sweepings from the streets of Plymouth) and 'point stuff' (stinking detritus from strand line of the tidal river) were sometimes combined to form a mucky fertiliser – nectar to Tamar Valley soil!

Above Tamar Valley daffodil pickers

Right The River Tamar

Salmon fishing

Salmon fishing in the Tamar has a long history. In 1356, 200 salted salmon were ordered by Edward, the Black Prince from his manor in Calstock. In 1759 Prince Edward, son of King George III and later Duke of York, went fishing on the Tamar with Richard 2nd Baron Edgcumbe (elder brother of 1st Earl) and caught 20 salmon.

Throughout the 20th century, fishing was carried out using nets stretched across the width of the river. As late as the 1990s, many local people supplemented their income with salmon from the river. Although the Tamar was full of toxins when copper mining was at its height in the 19th century, it wasn't until the latter half of the 20th century that stocks started to visibly dwindle. In 2004 Natural England put a ban on netting for salmon in the River Tamar, and paid fishermen a retainer not to net. For the time being, only line fishing is permitted.

Above Salmon fishing in the 1970s

Industry on the Tamar

In its 19th-century heyday, the Cotehele estate and surrounding Tamar Valley was a thriving industrial hub. The river was its highway. As well as market gardens and salmon fishing, lime burning and mining were major local industries.

Limekilns

Redundant limekilns, scattered along the riverbank, once burnt layers of limestone (from Plymouth) and coal, fed into the kiln from above, to produce lime. The burning process was highly skilled, unpleasant, smelly and slow. The processed lime was shovelled out of the small hearth and stored under arches to keep it dry, as it reacts violently when it comes into contact with water. It was never transported by river, but was taken short distances by horse and cart to be used as a fertilising agent by the market gardeners to neutralise the acid in the soil. It could also be used as an ingredient for paint (limewash) and as mortar for building.

Mining

The mineral-rich Tamar Valley has been exploited for centuries. Copper, arsenic, tin and silver lay hidden beneath the surface. From the late 19th century, Cornish mining spiralled into decline owing to mass emigration of skilled workers, and two World Wars. The ivy-clad ruins of engine houses strewn across the landscape serve as poignant reminders of vibrant industrial communities long since dispersed.

By 1290 and continuing into the late 19th century, silver and lead were mined on the area of land across the river from Cotehele Quay – the Bere Peninsula. In 1486 Richard Edgcumbe became Controller of the Mines Royal, a prestigious and profitable position.

His great-grandson, Piers, dabbled in speculative mining, but his ventures were unsuccessful and he accumulated huge debts.

Mining flourished in the Tamar Valley in the 19th century. Extraction was difficult and dangerous – the local churchyards are full of epitaphs mourning the loss of young men. Despite the fatality rate, the industry was attractive for skilled workers. The second half of the 19th century saw a steady migration of Cornish miners to distant lands, where many made their fortune. Popular destinations were the Americas, South Africa and Australia, where Cornish miners and their wives became known as 'Cousin Jack' and 'Cousin Jenny' respectively.

Cotehele Consols in Danescombe Valley was the nearest mine to Cotehele. Its engine house is now leased to the Landmark Trust, and is available as a holiday cottage. Two associated buildings, one an engine house and the other most likely used by the mines assayer, are National Trust holiday cottages. In 2006, the Cornwall and West Devon mining landscape, which includes Cotehele, gained World Heritage Site status.

Above Limestone from Plymouth at Cotehele Quay in late Victorian times, showing the limekilns in the background (Courtesy of the Earl of Mount Edgcumbe)

Nature notes
The limekilns are now of ecological rather than economic interest. Maidenhair ferns, more commonly seen in tropical rainforests of South America, festoon the curved walls of the dark, damp, lime-rich caverns.

Left The Tamar Valley near Cotehele, 1945. The mine buildings in the foreground are Cotehele Consols

Continuing Inspiration

Cotehele has a long history of inspiring poets, writers, musicians and artists. Here are just a few pictures by artists who were inspired by what they experienced at Cotehele.

Top *The Fugitive Jacobite* (showing Cotehele's Punch Room) by W. F. Yeames

Above *Wheels Within a Waterwheel* by Marie Martin

In the 1860s, a group of artists called the St John's Wood Clique are said to have stayed at Cotehele. **W. F. Yeames** (1835–1918) was a member of this group. He is most famous for painting *And When Did You Last See Your Father?* The title of his painting *The Fugitive Jacobite* is ironic as in 1745 Richard 1st Baron was commissioned to raise a regiment against the Jacobite uprising.

Rosamond Talbot (1837–1906) was the daughter of William Henry Fox Talbot and Lady Caroline's niece. Her sister, Matilda, created a watercolour of Cotehele's Hall in 1902.

Marie Martin née Langsford (b.1914) did not train as an artist, but she committed her memories to canvas throughout her life. Her

Above *The Porter's Lodge* by Rosamond Talbot

Opposite top *Cotehele Orchard by Moonlight* by Rena Gardiner

Opposite below *The Tower at Cotehele* by Mary Martin

daughter, **Mary Martin** (b.1951), trained in London for seven years as an artist, but apart from that has always lived in St Dominick. *The Tower at Cotehele* is one of the first paintings she created after returning to Cornwall on completion of her studies.

Rena Gardiner (1929–99) was an art teacher, artist, printmaker and writer. She also produced guidebooks for over 50 historic house, castles and churches, researching, writing and even printing them herself on her hand-operated press. Amongst them is *Look at Cotehele*, which has been reprinted for sale. In 1999 she held an exhibition at Cotehele of linocut prints inspired by the house and estate.

Cotehele today

Above **Cotehele seen from the south**

Cotehele is a truly special place that has played and continues to play an important part in many people's lives. Its atmosphere is deeply imbued with history, its views of the Tamar Valley are a joy and its tranquillity is much valued by the modern-day visitor.

A journey to Cotehele is always purposeful; it is a destination that sits discreetly on the banks of the River Tamar but firmly in Cornwall. It tells the story of the Edgcumbe family's country retreat and since the first foundations were laid over 600 years ago, Cotehele House, smelling of wood smoke and feeling 'authentic', has evolved to give a sense of timelessness.

Nestled within a once bountiful, industrial landscape, the Quay and Mill are evidence of a productive past. Market gardening played an important part in the valley's history and throughout the seasons, flowers continue to draw visitors to the garden, be it daffodils in the spring or the achievement of the garland in the winter.

Cotehele is a place where people feel a sense of peace and calm, somewhere they can disconnect from the pace of modern living. More than anything it is a happy place where memories are forged and imaginations cast.

Iain Beaumont, Cotehele General Manager, and team